Cassidy's Magic

JENNY WAGNER

ILLUSTRATED BY DIANE WORLAND

Cassidy's Magic

ISBN 13: 978-0-73-271545-8
ISBN 10: 0-73-271545-8

 **Kingscourt**

Published by:
McGraw-Hill Education
Shoppenhangers Road, Maidenhead, Berkshire, England, SL6 2QL
Telephone: 44 (0) 1628 502730
Fax: 44 (0) 1628 635895
Website: www.kingscourt.co.uk
Website: www.mcgraw-hill.co.uk

Written by **Jenny Wagner**
Illustrated by **Diane Worland**
Designedy by **Marina Messiha**

© 1995 Mimosa Publications
  Printed in 2009

All Rights reserved.

Printed in China

CONTENTS

◆

CHAPTER 1
Magic, Please! 5
◆
CHAPTER 2
Mud Soup 17
◆
CHAPTER 3
Vanishing Trick 29
◆
CHAPTER 4
Fish Milkshake 37
◆
CHAPTER 5
By Appointment Only 51
◆
CHAPTER 6
Photonic Energy 59
◆
CHAPTER 7
Important Warning 75
◆
CHAPTER 8
Payback 81

1

MAGIC, PLEASE!

There was a time when I was always looking for something magical. I knew all about magic rings, magic coins, talking fish, and genies in bottles, and just in case I ever found one, I had my three wishes ready.

But when something magical *did* happen to me, it wasn't the three wishes kind. Instead, one bright November afternoon, in the blink of an eye, I managed to wipe my parents, brother, aunty, uncle, best friend, and even my cat totally out of existence. And I wasn't even trying.

The whole thing began, as strange stories often do, on a rainy Friday evening in October. The house was a little neater than usual, and there was a fire blazing in the grate. (We didn't really need it but it looked more welcoming.) Sam was sprawled on the floor watching *Captain Amazing*, and Mephisto was draped over my shoulder, purring his evening purr as if nothing in the world was wrong.

But if I turned and looked past him, I could see the suitcases in the hall. They had appeared there very discreetly, as if our parents hoped we wouldn't notice: two big blue suitcases belonging to Mum and Dad, and a collection of bags and boxes belonging to Sam. Our parents' bags both had labels with their names, and the destination (*WIEN-VIENNA*) in big black letters. Sam's things had no labels. He was only going to the next suburb, to his friend Daniel's place. There was no luggage for me; I wasn't going anywhere. I had promised to stay home and look after Mephisto.

And somewhere overhead, on their way to look after me, were my aunty and uncle. Just about now their plane would be starting its descent, leaving a sky of hard bright stars and coming down into the murky drizzle of Harrietville. Before long a taxi would pull into our drive, and Aunty Mona and Uncle Frank would be here.

I was nervous about meeting them. We'd only met once before, and I was asleep in my cot at the time. But I supposed they must be nice – they were coming all this way just to look after me, weren't they?

I wondered if they'd bring a present or two. Mum had put flowers and chocolates in their

room, and when adults give each other presents there's usually something for the kids. Besides, I could tell that Aunty Mona and Uncle Frank were rich. The photo on the fridge showed a man and a woman about the same age as my parents, dressed in deck shoes, white shorts, and blue and white shirts. They looked very smart and nautical, as if they were about to go sailing, only there was no boat. There was just a vast sea of shaved green lawn around them. With a back yard that big they would have to be rich, wouldn't they?

The other good thing was that they had no children of their own, and for the next six weeks I was hoping to fill the gap. Whenever they felt the need to do something with their money, I'd be there to help them spend it.

A fragrant blue haze of hot oil and browned onions and potatoes was coming from the kitchen; Mum and Dad were busy making oozywotsits, mysterious little potato things that were said to be Aunty Mona's special favourite. They must have been difficult to make because Mum and Dad had been slaving in the kitchen all afternoon, grating, boiling, chopping, mashing, and frying. That was partly why dinner was so late. The other reason was that we had to wait for our visitors.

Sam has to be fed every sixty minutes or he implodes, and tonight he was already wobbly at the edges. *Captain Amazing* was over, and he was fiddling with the remote control, flicking the TV on and off to see who he could annoy.

He annoyed me. So I pinned him down on the couch and threatened him with the dreaded dog torture, where you get nuzzled all over if you don't behave.

"You're not mucking around in there, are you?" called Mum.

At that moment a taxi pulled into the drive.

Everyone knew who it was, but Sam hurled himself off the couch, knocking over the coffee table and the biscuits I'd arranged, and dashed into the kitchen shrieking, "They're here! They're here!"

I wondered how Daniel's family would cope with having Sam for a whole six weeks, and I wondered what I'd do if they tried to give him back early.

There was a knock at the door. Mephisto hissed, thrashed his tail, and ran off to the back of the house. I thought then that he was just annoyed at all the disturbance; but now I think that he must have known what was coming, because he didn't appear again for a whole day.

"Let them in, someone!" Dad yelled. "I can't leave the oozywotsits!"

"I can't let them in!" said Sam. "They've never seen me before. They'll think they've come to the wrong house."

The knock came again. "Cass!" shouted Mum. "Can't you?"

I didn't want to be the person to greet them either, but Sam is good at getting away with things. Already he had vaporized himself and was nowhere to be seen. So I opened the door.

The crumpled-looking couple on the porch looked older than the people in the photograph, and smaller, as if being away from their grand home had somehow made them less important. Or perhaps it was their clothes – they didn't

look rich and sporty any more. Uncle Frank was wearing a creased grey cardigan over baggy trousers, and Aunty Mona was wearing a pink acrylic cardigan over a dress covered with purple flowers. But in her hand was a raffia basket, and it was bulging. At least they had brought some presents.

I stood aside to let them in, and suddenly everybody was squeezing into the hallway, hugging and kissing and saying, "And how was your flight?" and "My, how you've grown", and "Is this *really* Cassidy?"

I was feeling embarrassed by all the attention and couldn't think of the proper grown-up thing to say, so I said, "Yes, apparently." It was meant to sound light and careless, but it came out sounding sarcastic. Aunty Mona gave me a funny look and put a cold kiss on my cheek.

Mum was looking a bit puzzled. "You and Frank have changed too, Mona. I almost wouldn't have known you," she said.

When all the greetings were over and the visitors' things had been put in their bedroom, we sat down to dinner. Dad sang out "Ta-da!" and Mum brought in the oozywotsits. She put the platter in front of Aunty Mona and stood back, smiling expectantly; I think she was waiting for Aunty Mona to say, "Oh, look, my special favourite!"

But nothing happened. Aunty Mona just looked at the brown, fritter-like things in front of her, poked them with her fork, and turned to Uncle Frank.

"Look, oozywotsits!" Dad said, nudging him and grinning.

Uncle Frank said, "Uh, we don't really eat that sort of stuff any more. We only eat healthy food now."

In spite of all those hours in the kitchen, Mum didn't turn a hair. She said, "That's all right, Frank", and passed them a big platter of sliced ham. But they stared at that, too.

"Come on," Dad said. "It's good ham. The best you can get."

"It's the preservatives," Uncle Frank said. "They poison your system. Did you know that buried corpses take longer to decay these days, because they're so full of preservatives?"

I wanted to know more about that, but suddenly Dad started talking about the new baby next door. Then they all got on to car prices and real estate, and nobody said anything interesting any more. Sam and I ate the extra ham and oozywotsits, and Aunty Mona and Uncle Frank had a salad for dinner. Or rather, they had just plain lettuce, because they didn't like the salad dressing, either.

When the plates were cleared away Aunty Mona opened her raffia basket. I was holding my breath in expectation, and I could see that Sam felt the same way – his mouth was gaping open like an old sock.

But there was nothing in the basket except two empty lunch boxes and a thermos flask. "You children won't mind washing these lunch things, will you?" Aunty Mona said. "We took our own food on the plane. You just can't trust the meals they give you."

"The food at airports poisons your system, too," Uncle Frank said. "And the prices are highway robbery."

Mum clucked sympathetically and asked if anyone would like some ice-cream.

I was still feeling disappointed that there'd been nothing nice in Aunty Mona's raffia basket, but I didn't want to show it in case she thought I was badly brought up. So when ice-cream was mentioned, I made a special effort to look happy. But I overdid it. "Ooh!" I squealed dramatically. "Ice-cream! I could kill for some ice-cream!"

Even as I said it I realized just how silly it sounded, and wished I'd kept my mouth shut. Aunty Mona gave me a long, serious look over the top of her glasses. "Cassidy!" she said. "I'm sure you don't mean that."

Of course I didn't mean it. It was a figure of speech. "No, not really," I mumbled.

Normally I stay up as late as I can get away with, but tomorrow Mum and Dad were leaving, and I wanted the comfort of my bed. I wanted to curl up under the blankets with Mephisto and tell myself that six weeks wasn't long. But Mephisto was still hiding, so I curled up under the blankets alone.

There was a tap at the door, and Mum came in. "Hi, Chicken Casserole. You okay?" She sat down on the bed. "You're not having second thoughts, are you?"

Of course I was! When I agreed to stay and mind Mephisto, I was expecting to be looked after by a rich aunty and uncle like the ones you see in movies. I expected the sort of uncle who laughed a lot and gave you the loose change from his pockets. I expected an aunty who fluttered around in coffee-coloured silk and said things like, "Here, darling, you'd better have this emerald brooch. It doesn't go with my new shoes."

But somehow I was stuck with the sort who carried a cut lunch onto a plane, drank weak herbal tea instead of coffee, and were so mean they didn't even bring a bag of jelly beans. But I didn't know how to say it without sounding greedy. So I said nothing at all.

"I know Mona and Frank aren't quite what we expected, but they'll take good care of you. If you were really upset – if you were really, really unhappy, I could stay home, too."

I wanted to say, "Yes, stay home!" but I couldn't. It was too late for that. There'd be a huge upheaval and it would be all my fault. On top of that, I would have to admit that I wasn't as grown-up as I'd pretended.

"No, it's okay," I mumbled. And because at moments like this I tend to overdo things, I added with an air of self-sacrifice, "You enjoy your trip. Really, there's nothing to worry about. I'll be quite all right. Honest."

I didn't mean it, of course. What I really thought was that only magic could save me from six weeks of misery. Little did I know that magic *was* on the way – and it was bringing trouble with it!

2

MUD SOUP

On Saturdays I usually like to stay in bed for a while. But today, even though it was windy and rainy, I got up early. I wanted to squeeze every last minute out of the time left with Mum and Dad. For the next couple of hours, Sam and I had them more or less to ourselves; Aunty Mona and Uncle Frank had gone shopping – they hadn't been able to find anything in the house that was healthy enough for them.

Sam and I trailed after Mum and Dad while they rushed about banging doors and shouting things like, "What about the keys?" and "Did you remember to call the bank?" It was almost as if they didn't live here any more. They didn't even mind how cold the house was. "It's not worth turning the heating on," said Dad. "We'll be going soon."

Uncle Frank and Aunty Mona came back with recycled bags full of stuff from the health food shop, and Aunty Mona made breakfast.

Mum and Dad didn't have time to eat and I didn't really want anything either. But when I saw the trouble she'd gone to, even putting a cloth on the kitchen table, I gave in and said I'd just have some muesli.

But it wasn't the toasty, crunchy stuff we usually have – Sam had finished that. This was something especially awful that Aunty Mona made herself, out of chopped straw with a handful of cement dust thrown in.

Mephisto was still in hiding, so I couldn't give him his breakfast. He hadn't come near me all night and I really missed him; it was the first night he hadn't slept with me since he was a kitten.

We drove to the airport in Dad's car, and Mum sat in the back with Sam and me. "If you really miss us," she said to me, "you can call the hotel. And we'll call you sometimes, too."

All this talk about missing them was making me weepy. Aunty Mona and Uncle Frank seemed so stiff, so cold, not like Mum and Dad.

"Dad and I will write to you every week," Mum said, "but just remember we're travelling, so some letters might take a while."

With a sudden lurch of panic I said, "What if something bad happens? What if I really need you, and no one knows where you are?"

Dad gave me a hug. "Frank and Mona will always know how to find us."

We sat around for ages at the airport while Mum and Dad stood in lines. At one stage there was a delay while a woman in uniform checked something, and for a wild, joyful moment I thought she was going to say, "I'm sorry, your papers aren't in order; you'll have to stay behind." But she didn't.

Dad bought hot fudge sundaes to cheer us up, and then it was time to say good-bye. We hugged and kissed and I tried not to cry. Mum and Dad left very quickly; Mum's mouth was crumpling into funny shapes, and Dad was brushing his hand over his eyes.

I don't know what they had to cry about – they would be getting all the fun. Unless, like Mephisto, they somehow knew what was coming.

At the last moment, Mum called, "Cass! Your pocket money – I've left it with Aunty Mona!"

And Dad said, "Enjoy yourselves! See you in six weeks!"

Then they were gone. I bawled in earnest now. So did Sam – but not as loudly or as long as I did, because at least he was going to his friend's place. I was the one staying with Aunty Mona and Uncle Frank.

Aunty Mona put her skinny arms around us and said, "It's not as if you're all alone – you've got *us*!" I didn't want to hurt her feelings so I gave her a little hug, but she felt hard and bony, not like our mum at all.

On the way home I was expecting that we'd stop somewhere for a hamburger or pizza for lunch. It would cheer us up to do something special, and that's the sort of thing Mum and Dad would have done.

But it wasn't the sort of thing our aunty and uncle did. It didn't even occur to them, and when I suggested it, Uncle Frank said, "No, no, Cassidy, not with the prices those places charge. There's plenty of healthy food at home." That was what I was afraid of.

We dropped Sam off at Daniel's place, then headed home. I thought, never mind – there'll be pizza another day. To fill up the time I'd feed Mephisto. Then I'd call Vanessa and ask her to come over.

Vanessa is my best friend. The only reason Mephisto and I were staying at my place and not hers was that her sister was getting married, and their house was full of bridesmaids, pink satin and relatives.

When we got home the house looked very bare. Usually our living room has a squashy, round kind of look. But now that everyone had put away their odds and ends, the room seemed angular and cold.

"I'm freezing," I said.

"I'm sure we don't need the heat on," said Aunty Mona.

"You'll soon warm up if you move around," said Uncle Frank. "You can help your aunty with the lunch."

"No, I like to do the cooking myself," said Aunty Mona. "But Cassidy can vacuum the living room if she likes."

Vacuum the living room? If I like? I'd just lost both my parents. I was in no state to work.

At that moment, Mephisto came out of his hiding place and started weaving around my legs, meowing to be fed.

"I didn't know you had a cat," said Uncle Frank, holding the back door open.

I didn't realize why he was holding it open, and I went on getting Mephisto's food out of the fridge and putting it in his bowl. Then Aunty Mona said, "Well, come on, Cassidy. Put your cat outside."

"Oh, no," I explained. "Mephisto gets fed in here. He has his own place – look." And I showed them how he ran to his special corner when he saw that his breakfast was ready.

Uncle Frank gave a knowing chuckle. "Oho, Cassidy! We may not have any children, but we know the tricks they get up to. I'm sure you're not allowed to have the cat in the house. We've

been here since last night – and we haven't seen it once until now!"

I tried to protest, but they wouldn't listen. Still laughing, Aunty Mona picked Mephisto up, dropped him outside, and shut the door behind him. He began to wail like a lost kitten.

I snatched his breakfast and ran after him. I was furious. Not so much because Aunty Mona was making me feed him outside – he was hungry enough not to care about that – but because this was *my* house, and she'd grabbed hold of my cat, without caring how he felt, and without listening to me. It was as if she'd dumped *me* outside.

I fed Mephisto on my windowsill and left

the window open for him. There was no way I'd make him stay outside, and at night I'd make sure he was safely shut in my room. Cats belong indoors at night.

I thought my aunty and uncle would never find out that Mephisto was living in my room – not unless they went in there, and I was sure they'd never do that. Not even Sam was game to go into my bedroom. There were big signs on the door warning people off:

DANGER
RADIOACTIVE SOCKS
DEFINITELY KEEP OUT
NO ONE ALOUD WITHOUT PERMISSION
(I was going to fix that one day.)
THIS MEANS YOU! and so on.

As soon as I'd finished feeding Mephisto, I called Vanessa's. The whole empty afternoon was stretching in front of me; I needed her to come over. We could hire a video game. I wouldn't even have minded one of Sam's computer games – except that he'd taken all the disks. But Vanessa wasn't home – she'd gone to be measured for her bridesmaid's dress.

But I wouldn't let myself be disappointed. There were six weeks of this emptiness in front of me, and it was no good falling apart on the first day. Instead, I'd get my pocket money from Aunty Mona and pick up some videos to watch. I'd put the old video-TV in my room, curl up under the quilt with Mephisto, and we'd watch comedies together. And soon, *one* day out of the forty-two would be over.

"Lunch-time!" called Aunty Mona. "Come and see what I've made for you!"

As I sat down at the table Uncle Frank said, "You're very lucky, Cassidy. Your aunty's a wonderful cook." He nodded at the steaming bowl of brown, muddy stuff that Aunty Mona had put in front of me. "And everything she makes is so healthy."

"Every single ingredient in this soup is good for you," Aunty Mona said. "And there are twenty-one of them."

I tasted the soup. "Can I have some salt?"

Aunty Mona said, "It has sardines, broccoli, anchovies, spinach, cauliflower, mushrooms, cabbage, soybeans, brussels sprouts, cloves, alfalfa, sauerkraut, garlic, lentils and lots of other good things. When you have all those healthy ingredients, you certainly don't need to add salt."

I tasted the soup again – I just had to, I was starving – and decided that maybe she was right. Without salt, you couldn't taste very much at all.

But a more cheerful thought had occurred to me. On the way to the video shop I would pass Max's Hot Dogs. I could get some videos and something good to eat at the same time. "Aunty Mona," I said, "can I have my pocket money today, please?"

"Of course, dear," said Aunty Mona. "How much would you like? I mean, what do you need to buy?"

My stomach sank. I might have guessed it would be like this. "I haven't made up my mind. I'd just like to have it, that's all."

Aunty Mona wagged her head at me. "Oh dear, no. Your mother gave *me* your pocket money so you wouldn't spend it on silly things. If you need books for school, or something important like that, all you have to do is ask."

I sat looking at my soup while I thought what to do. It was a Saturday afternoon – I could hardly tell her I needed it for school books. I stared at the soup so long that the muddy bits sank to the bottom, leaving the watery part on top. It looked like a puddle – I half expected to see mosquitoes breeding in it.

"Eat up, it's getting cold," said Uncle Frank.

I said, "I need pencils and stuff." It was true.

I always need pencils and erasers – I take after Dad. I keep losing them.

Aunty Mona gave me two dollars – not as much as I'd hoped for, but at least I could buy something to eat, and I'd be out of the house for a while. But if I'd known what was going to happen, I would certainly have stayed at home.

3

VANISHING TRICK

Hale Street was several blocks away, not far from my school. There was a row of shops, and on the corner was one where they sold fantastic hot dogs.

As I said at the beginning, I often used to wish that my life was more exciting – that one day something truly magical would happen to me. Up till now, nothing had. So when my need for some magic became unbearable, I used to pretend instead. I would kid myself that when Mephisto meowed, he was actually talking to me; or that when Sam's remote control plane went by it really had tiny people in it.

Vanessa, if she was around, would play along. Sometimes we'd go to the supermarket, and if I said, "Look, two aliens are pushing that shopping cart," she'd say, "Watch out for the death ray in the broccoli!" Then we'd follow the aliens back to their UFO, which always took off just before we got there.

I really wished Vanessa was with me now, because when I arrived at the hot dog shop I found that an unexpected thing had happened: someone had taken it away.

I know that in the middle of the night they sometimes take buildings and put them some place else. But those buildings are made of wood, and they're old. They're also empty. But the hot dog shop had been made of brick and was almost new, and until yesterday you could still buy hot dogs in it.

Now where it had stood there was just empty ground, with long grass and weeds growing over it. Nothing was left of Max's Hot Dogs: no rubble or broken timber, not even a paper wrapper – nothing to show that there had ever been a shop there at all.

I wondered if somehow I'd taken a wrong turning and ended up on a different street. But everything else was the same: there was Country Garden Dried Flowers; beside that was Lady-in-Waiting Maternity Wear; and next to that was Follansbee Fine Furniture Restoration, with its single, worm-eaten chair in the window. (Everyone knew that Mr Follansbee drilled the worm holes himself – I suppose real worms would have taken too long.) All the right shops were there – except for Max's Hot Dogs.

This was definitely the most magical thing that had happened to me in my entire life. I couldn't wait to tell Vanessa. I'd go to her house right away, and wait for her to come home.

"I expect it's those aliens again," I'd say.

And she'd say, "They've probably beamed the shop up to their ship. Sometimes they do that when they need a lot of hot dogs. They must be having a party."

That way I could enjoy some magic for a while, and maybe Vanessa's mum would feed me as well. They always have wonderful food at Vanessa's place.

I had to wait a while for Vanessa to come home, and her mum gave me a salami and pickle sandwich in the meantime.

When Vanessa finally showed up, pink-faced and excited, I tried to tell her about the amazing thing that had happened. But she wasn't even listening.

"My bridesmaid dress," she said dreamily, "is just the most incredible thing you ever saw. It's made of this pink, fluffy stuff with little roses all around, and it comes down to here, and there'll be little roses in my hair, and I'll have curls sort of like this . . ."

"Vanessa!" I yelled. "I've got something amazing to show you!"

Eventually I had to take her arm and drag her to Hale Street.

"See that?" I said as we reached the corner. "The hot dog shop has vanished."

"What hot dog shop?" Vanessa said.

"The one that isn't there any more." I can be very patient when I have to.

But even as I spoke, I could see that things weren't right. In fact, if things had been a bit odd before, now they were very, very wrong.

It was starting to get dark, but there was still enough light to see that there was a shop on the corner after all. It just wasn't the right one. It should have been a yellow brick building with "Max's Famous Hot Dogs" in red letters across the window. Or else it should have been a vacant lot.

This was a derelict wooden building. Paint was flaking off the fraying boards, the windows were white with dust, and weeds and grass grew around the doorway. On the cracked glass door I could just make out the ghostly letters of a sign: "WALT . . .OWL . ., Elec.ronic .upplies and R.pa.rs." Below the sign hung a card with "Closed" written on it.

"So?" said Vanessa. "There's an empty shop here. It's always been here. They're going to pull it down one day."

"But it used to be Max's Hot Dogs!" I said. "Don't you remember? Now it's a completely different shop – and it belongs to Walt Owl."

"No," said Vanessa flatly.

It was starting to rain. I argued. I couldn't believe Vanessa was doing this – I thought she was just in a bad mood because the rain was making her hair flat. I kept reminding her of the times we'd eaten hot dogs after school.

But she wouldn't listen. She insisted there'd never been a Max's Hot Dogs, ever.

Then she said something that really annoyed me. "Look, I'm getting wet. And I don't want to do that magic stuff any more. It's babyish."

She ran off home. I watched her disappear into the rain, and decided that all that fluffy pink stuff must have gone to her brain.

It was dark by the time I got home. I was worried about what Uncle Frank and Aunty Mona would say – I hadn't meant to be away that long.

They weren't very pleased at all. "I think, Cassidy," said Uncle Frank, "you owe your aunty an apology."

"Oh, Cassidy!" said Aunty Mona. "We've been so worried – we were about to call the police! I cooked such a lovely dinner for you, and you weren't here!"

I said I was sorry and went to the kitchen to get my dinner. I could smell something strange. I sniffed the air, trying to work out where it was coming from.

It turned out to be coming from the oven. "Cabbage and sardine stew," said Aunty Mona. "My specialty – and I only cook it on special occasions."

"And now it's nearly ruined," said Uncle Frank.

I sniffed the lumpy grey mush on my plate and knew that I'd come home too soon. I should have waited until it was completely ruined.

4

FISH MILKSHAKE

The next day it didn't stop raining. I tried to cheer myself up by calling Vanessa, but no one was home. I couldn't even watch TV: there was nothing on except programmes about gardening, cooking, and wild animals that had lost their habitats.

"We could play a game, couldn't we?" said Aunty Mona, putting a cardboard box on the coffee table.

Inside the box was something about the size of a video game, and for one wonderful moment that's what I thought it was. But no. This box was full of educational games – the sort that are meant to teach you things instead of entertain you. They had names like Thrift!, Str-e-tch Your Money, and Test Your Investment.

We played Thrift! for plastic counters, just like little kids, and it was the most boring game in the entire world. Aunty Mona and Uncle Frank were experts. They saved up their plastic

counters, bought lots of real estate, and won all my plastic counters. Then they loaned me more counters at huge interest and won all those, too. I lost every single game.

"Well," said Uncle Frank, when they were tired of beating me, "you have a lot to learn about managing money, don't you?"

I muttered something about not having any to practise with, but he didn't seem to hear.

"The first thing to know about money," said Uncle Frank, "is neither a borrower nor a lender be. The second thing is that everything in this life has to be paid for. Take what you want, and pay for it. That's what we say, right, Mona?"

And Aunty Mona, who had gone out to the kitchen to prepare another dreadful meal, called back, "Yes, Cassidy, that's our motto."

Maybe I should have listened to them; it would have saved a lot of misery later on. But it was all so depressing – the dark day, the rain pelting down outside, and Aunty Mona in the kitchen, chopping up something hard and cold for dinner. I daydreamed.

I imagined finding a magic machine that would grant me wishes and instantly turn me into a billionaire. I'd live in a huge mansion, and I'd let my aunty and uncle (who'd suddenly become very poor) work for me as my butler and ... well, maybe not as my cook.

Our dinner was cold brown rice, lettuce, raw spinach, raw brussels sprouts, and – surprise, surprise – sardines.

"Aunty Mona," I said, as I helped her put it on the table, "would you like me to make some custard for dessert? I know how."

"Custard poisons your system," said Uncle Frank. "It's the chemicals in the milk."

"But you can make us a cup of chamomile tea," said Aunty Mona. "That's much healthier."

In bed that night, I curled up with Mephisto and thought about Mr Walt Owl's shop. It seemed to me it must be there for a reason, if only I could work out what it was. That's how it goes with magic – everything fits together somehow, as long as you have the key.

On my way to school the next morning, I went past the shop again, but in the daylight it was disappointingly ordinary. It was just like any other run-down building. The glass on the door was still cracked, and the sign on it still said "Closed". There was nothing magical about the place at all.

I was hoping to go back right after school to have another look, but as it turned out I had an appointment with the principal. Aunty Mona had insisted on making my lunch for me, and at lunch-time the principal had caught me trying to ditch it.

That was after I'd tried to swap it with Pete Samson. Pete had a taste for rare, strange and unpleasant food. It was common knowledge that he ate anything. But not even he would eat my lunch. Aunty Mona had given me what seemed like dog biscuits, stuck together with sardine paste and chopped garden weeds. "No," said Pete when I offered it to him. "No – I won't take it from you. It wouldn't be fair."

So I didn't see the shop again until after school, and I couldn't help noticing that it

looked a little neater. The windows were still covered with dust, and the "Closed" sign still hung on the door. But the cracked glass had been replaced, and the weeds had disappeared from around the doorway.

I didn't say anything to Vanessa – I didn't

want to start a quarrel, but I made up my mind to wait and watch. For the next two weeks I went past the shop twice a day, checking to see how it was going, and each day it was a little less untidy. Bit by bit, the weeds disappeared, and the windows got cleaner. Then one day I saw that the walls had been painted.

Even Vanessa noticed that. "Good," she said. "They're not tearing it down after all. It's about time someone fixed it up."

It seemed to me that the shop was preparing itself for a particular kind of magic – its own kind of magic, whatever that was. But I didn't mention that to Vanessa either. Her head was still stuffed full of weddings, and she would only have found a reasonable explanation.

Besides, I needed her to go on being my friend, especially as far as food was concerned. There was just nothing in my house to eat. On the kitchen bench was a jar with more of the dog biscuits; next to it was Aunty Mona's straw and cement muesli. The refrigerator was full of weedy greens and hairy, sprouting things; the cupboards were full of dull grey powders and shrivelled, black lumpy things.

And there were sardines. Everywhere I looked, crammed into every possible space left over, were cans and cans of sardines.

Because Vanessa is my best friend, she started off by sharing her lunches with me. But Vanessa's lunches weren't enough for both of us, and after a few days she was as hungry as I was. So she started spending her pocket money on extra food.

For a couple of weeks we lived quite well on Vanessa's money. Every lunch-time, she bought ice-cream and apples and things at the school cafeteria, and shared them with me.

I kept promising I'd pay back what she spent on me. But as the days went by, Vanessa seemed to be spending more and more. The trouble was that I was too hungry to say no, and anyway, Vanessa was enjoying all the food as much as I was.

But one day I started adding it all up, and I realized that at this rate I could never pay her back.

Another of Uncle Frank's favourite sayings was, "You get nothing for nothing in this life. If you want something, you have to work for it."

So I weeded the garden and washed the windows, then showed him what I'd done.

"Good," he said. "Very good."

"Can you pay me?" I said. "I'll do it every week if you like."

Uncle Frank looked hurt. "That's not nice, Cassidy – expecting to be paid for every little thing you do. You should do these things for nothing, out of gratitude. Do you have any idea of what it costs to feed you?"

I thought Vanessa probably did.

To make things easier for her, I sometimes begged for food from other friends. They were kind to me, too – they would give me corners of their sandwiches, or bits of their apples.

But it was embarrassing, always taking things from friends and never being able to pay them back. Any day now, I thought, they'll have had enough of me. One day they'll see me coming, and quietly disappear.

More and more, magic seemed the only answer. I looked out for empty bottles and checked them for genies. I kept my eyes open, hoping for talking fish and magic coins – even an ordinary coin would have come in handy. But I didn't find a single thing.

Then one day Vanessa said, "Are you sure your lunch is so terrible? Lots of people have fish for lunch. You haven't even tried to like yours."

I handed her my lunchbox. It had the usual dog biscuits in it, but today they were stuck together with sardines, a pale paste made from cauliflower and brussels sprouts, and lots and lots of garlic.

Vanessa slammed the box shut. "Well, maybe today isn't the best day to start."

That afternoon Vanessa came to my place. She said she wanted to borrow my book on great wonders of the world, but there seemed to be something else on her mind. I thought she might be checking up on me, seeing if my aunty and uncle were as bad as I said. I didn't mind. I wanted her to see for herself, and to feel sorry for me.

Aunty Mona seemed pleased that I'd brought a friend home. "Nice to meet you, Vanessa!" she said. "Let me make you a milkshake."

I shook my head at Vanessa. "No, don't!" I whispered. "It's not a good idea. Believe me."

Vanessa took no notice. "Thank you, Aunt Mona," she said in her best-behaviour voice.

Aunty Mona put banana, soy milk, and honey in the blender, and Vanessa gave me an "I told you so" look.

As I passed the kitchen on my way to get the book, Aunty Mona beckoned me. "I'd normally put in some cod-liver oil," she said, "but it's so expensive. Do you think Vanessa will mind a substitute?"

"Of course not," I said.

A minute later Vanessa was standing at my bedroom door, her face as white as a sheet. "You won't believe this," she whispered. There was a moustache of white froth on her top lip. "Your aunty just made me a fish milkshake."

Then she rushed off down the hall. I poured the milkshake into Mephisto's dish, but he didn't want it either.

Vanessa came back and sat on my bed for a while, glancing through *Great Wonders of the World*. Then she untied both her shoes and tied them again, and compared the length of her fingernails.

Then she said, "Why don't you call Sam and see if he's got any money?"

So that was it: Vanessa wanted me to start paying her back. This was the moment I'd been dreading. I hadn't thought of asking Sam for a loan – he spends his money as soon as he gets it, so there was no point. But now that Vanessa had asked, the least I could do was try. I called from the phone in my parents' bedroom.

"I didn't want to ask you," Vanessa said, trailing in after me, "but I've been spending the money in my savings – you know, the money I was supposed to be keeping for holidays. And

now my parents have found out. I got into big trouble."

Sam answered the phone. Without messing around, I asked him for some of his pocket money.

"I can't. I've spent it," he said.

"Next week, then. Save me as much as you can. It's urgent!"

"I mean I've spent all of it. Daniel's mum gave me the whole six weeks' worth in one lot, and you know what I'm like with money. Listen, I can't talk any more now – we're all going out for hamburgers."

I yelled at him. I roared. I called him greedy for living on hamburgers while I starved, and for being showered with money while I scraped by on a measly two dollars. And I called him selfish and mean for taking the games disks with him. Then I burst into tears.

Sam was silent all through my speech. Then he said, "Gee, I'm sorry. I didn't know." I could hear voices in the background calling him to hurry up. "I'm sorry," Sam said again. "I've got to go." And he hung up.

Vanessa handed me her pink handkerchief.

"Let's go to your place," I said, sniffling.

"Well..."

Vanessa seemed a little uncomfortable about something, but I was too hungry to pay much attention. I wanted to get a sandwich – I loved the way they made sandwiches at Vanessa's place – and then I wanted to look at Walt Owl's Magic Shop, in case something amazing had happened.

Just as we were leaving the house, Uncle Frank handed me a postcard. "I nearly forgot – this came for you today. You're a very lucky girl – you're the only person who got one."

The postcard was from my parents. "That should make you happy!" said Aunty Mona.

And it did – until I read it.

5

BY APPOINTMENT ONLY

Vanessa didn't say a word to me as we walked toward her house. I thought she was just letting me read my postcard in peace – it certainly needed some working out. It was in Mum's big writing, though she had written smaller to fit more on. But she hadn't left enough room for the stamps. They were very big, and there were a lot of them. To fit them on, someone had stuck them all down the side, and now they covered up chunks of the writing.

The message looked like this:

*Hello darling! The weather has been so that we decided to change our plans and go to where we hope to stay for at least another Then if the weather's all right we'll go to and after that, if we can manage to get we hope to venture into the wilds of So that's our new itinerary! That means we might be home a bit than expected. Don't worry! We'll be Hope that's okay with you.
Love and kisses,
Mum and Dad.*

It was definitely not okay with me. What did they mean by "Don't worry?" Where were they going – the Bermuda Triangle? And where were they now? The picture showed buildings, palm trees, and a sapphire blue sky, and underneath were the words "The main business district: the view from the beach". What beach? Even the stamps were no help. The part that showed what country they came from had been covered up with a black, blurry postmark.

"Don't worry," Vanessa said. "Postcards always have palm trees on them. Even if they come from Iceland, they show you palm trees. Your mum and dad could have sent that from anywhere."

"Thanks a lot," I said.

We were getting close to the shop, and Vanessa had that hesitant air again, as if she wanted to say something but couldn't quite remember it. Then when we were in sight of the Magic Shop she said suddenly, "I think I'll go home now. I expect you'd rather stay here, wouldn't you?"

"No, I want to go to your place – I'm really starving."

Vanessa was silent for a long time, and I had a dreadful feeling that I knew exactly what was coming. At last she said, "When I got into trouble for spending my money, I said I spent it all on you."

"Gee, that was big of you."

"I didn't know what else to say. I was in big trouble – I had to blame someone." Vanessa leaned against the wall of the Magic Shop, hugging her backpack to her chest, and stared at her feet – her pink and white tennis shoes seemed to be shuffling about on the pavement all by themselves. "I tried to tell Mum and Dad your aunty and uncle were starving you, but they wouldn't believe me. So now you're not allowed at our place till you've paid me back."

I leaned against the wall next to Vanessa. Now my feet were shuffling, too, and my face burned with anger and shame.

"I've got to go," Vanessa said. "I'll be late for dinner." But maybe she thought that wasn't the most tactful thing to say, because then she said, "I'm sorry. It'll be all right. You can still share my lunch tomorrow."

She went home, and I stood for a long time staring at Owl's Magic Shop. I felt as if I'd been caught with my hand in someone's purse. It was high time for some magic in my life.

The luminous evening arched overhead and a soft, papery moon appeared. The windows of the Magic Shop glimmered in the dusk. Dozens of times I'd looked in those windows and seen nothing but dust and dead flies. Now I saw that someone had arranged a display.

Against a background of TVs and videos there was a row of boxes, each one the size of a video game. And even though I couldn't make out the labels, my highly developed sense of the amazing told me that these were no ordinary boxes. These were the magical sort that granted wishes.

Then I noticed that underneath the "Closed" sign another sign had appeared, painted on to the glass in small red letters. In the last of the rosy light I could just read the words: "Hours by Appointment Only."

My heart stood still. Of course! How else would you get into a Magic Shop? I hunted through my pockets for something to write with, and finally found a chocolate wrapper and one of Dad's scratchy pencils.

I wrote: "I would like an appointment for tomorrow (Friday) afternoon after school, please. Thank you, Yours faithfully, Cassidy."

In the pale light the pencil hardly made a mark on the paper, but I persevered, going over and over the letters till they were dark enough to read. Then I pushed the note under the door.

When I got home Aunty Mona said, "Your brother was here with his little friend. They left you something."

Just outside my bedroom door was the box of games disks. A note on top said, "Look inside", and squeezed in among the disks I found an oval carton that used to be square. It was a slightly squashed hamburger from Emperor Burgers. Under the carton was an envelope with ten dollars in it.

My first thought was to take the hamburger into a corner and devour it. But then I thought it might be nicer warmed up, so I put it in the microwave instead.

"You're not eating that now, are you?" said Aunty Mona. "You'll spoil your dinner. I've cooked you chilli con sardines!"

But nothing could have kept me from that hamburger. I took it into my bedroom, gave

Mephisto a tiny piece and wolfed the rest down; the juice trickled down my chin and all over my fingers. Nothing had ever tasted so good. Before I went to bed that night I called Sam to thank him, but he and Daniel were still out at the movies.

As I lay in the dark thinking, it seemed that the power of Owl's Magic Shop was already working. Weren't the money and the hamburger proof of that? Tomorrow I would take my ten dollars to the Magic Shop and buy one of the games that granted wishes. Then everything would be all right. I was sure of it.

6

PHOTONIC ENERGY

The next morning, I folded Sam's money into a hard little lump. I was about to put it into my pocket when Uncle Frank said, "Well, Cassidy, have you been saving?"

"Um, there's something I need to buy," I said.

Uncle Frank shook his head. "It's just as well we're keeping the rest of your pocket money safe. I can't understand you young people; as soon as you get money, you have to spend it. You know the saying: *Take what you want and pay for it.* You'll end up paying, you'll see."

I wasn't sure what he meant. It sounded vaguely ominous, but then most of Uncle Frank's sayings were like that, so I didn't take much notice.

I kept the money in my pocket all day. Every so often I rolled it around in my fingers, and thought of my appointment at the Magic Shop. I felt a little guilty about not giving some of it to

Vanessa, but now that real magic was within my grasp, I knew what I had to do. I'd been waiting for this opportunity all my life; in one of those boxes was the answer to all my problems.

I expected the shop to be like one of those antique shops in the movies. You know the kind: a nice old gentleman sells someone a rare artifact, a hand-carved box, perhaps, for hardly any money – usually for the exact money in your pocket. Then later on you find out that it grants wishes. This means that you have to be very careful. In some movies I've seen, the thing starts granting wishes before you even know you've wished them.

All day long I thought about how good it would be to get my parents home, to send Aunty Mona and Uncle Frank back to where they belonged, and to have roast chicken with gravy and mashed potatoes for dinner. I was looking forward to paying Vanessa what I owed her, and having her parents think I was a decent person again.

And I thought how nice it would be to have Vanessa stay over at my place. On a windy Friday night, with the rain drumming on the roof, we'd curl up on the couch with Mephisto, drink hot chocolate, watch videos, and eat pizza and cheesecake.

I was expecting Vanessa to walk down Hale Street with me after school, but as we went out of the school gate she said, "I'm not going that way. The wedding's tomorrow – I've got to go to a rehearsal."

A rehearsal? The most important chance of our lives, and she was going to a wedding rehearsal? What was there to rehearse, besides walking and standing still?

I tried to persuade her. I tried to tell her about my appointment, and how I was going to get a magic box that would be the answer to all our dreams. But Vanessa, her head still full of satin and pink roses, said, "Cassidy, you can be so childish at times."

So I had to go to the Magic Shop by myself.

When I got there the "Closed" sign was on the door. I tried the handle, but it was locked. I didn't let that stop me – I knew it was just to keep other people out. Politely, I tapped on the door and waited for someone to open it. No one came. I knocked again, and still no one came. I peered in through the window, but the shop was as deserted as yesterday.

I thought perhaps I'd arrived too early. I hadn't put any special time on my note, and I guess "after school" could mean a lot of different things. So I waited.

But then, as the minutes passed and still there was no sign of movement, I felt a stirring of disappointment, even doubt. I wondered if I'd been kidding myself again.

If so, I was in serious trouble. I still owed Vanessa money, and my parents were still missing. There was a good chance I'd be stuck with Aunty Mona and Uncle Frank, two dollars a month to live on, and sardines, spinach and shell grit until I was old enough to vote.

It was that thought that made me knock on the door again, banging and shouting to make myself heard. And this time I saw a movement inside; at the back of the shop someone was pointing at the window.

I stood back and looked. Painted on the glass in large red letters there was yet another sign: "Appointments, please use other door." A large red arrow pointed round the corner. I'd never noticed the door on Dracott Street before, but there it was, glistening with fresh green paint. And it was open.

The shop was darker inside than I expected. I waited a few moments, and gradually I made out the outline of another doorway. A limp brown curtain hung in front of it.

"Hello?" I called. "Is anyone there? Mr Owl?"

"Rowley!" came a gruff voice from behind the curtain. "Name's Rowley! What are you standing out there for? The shop's in here!"

I pushed through the curtain and found myself in the Owl Magic Shop. The old man was just as ancient as I'd expected, but nowhere near as good tempered.

"Well?" he said. "What is it?"

I didn't know what to say. He was in charge of the magic – I thought he would know. "I've come for my appointment," I said at last.

"I know that, stupid child! What did you want an appointment for?"

Wasn't this the part where I told him all my troubles? I thought I'd skip that. When you tell your troubles to someone, you like to feel they're interested.

I looked at the boxes in the window. The sun had bleached the printed lids into brown and yellow blotches, so there was no way of telling what was in them. "What are they?" I asked. "I mean – "

He didn't let me finish. "Specials."

"But what sort?"

"How would I know? That's why they're specials."

I supposed that in a magic shop "specials" and "special" must mean much the same thing.

But this wasn't going the way I'd expected. He was meant to open a box, show me a magic video game worth hundreds of dollars, then sell it to me for ten.

"Are you going to stand there all day?" he said. "Make up your mind. Take what you want, and pay for it."

The words stirred up an eddy of doubt in my mind. They were exactly what Uncle Frank said, but now they seemed even more ominous.

But I'd come too far to turn back. I took a box from the middle of the row. "I'll have this one."

"Thirty dollars," he said.

"Thirty?" I stood there with my mouth open, the box in one hand and my ten dollars in the other. This part wasn't in the script either.

"Thirty," he said again. "Hurry up."

"I've only got ten."

"You want me to give it to you, is that it? You ask me for an appointment – a favour – then expect me to give you whatever you ask for, like a genie out of a bottle?"

"No, no. I just want to buy something for ten dollars."

He thrust his ancient turtle-face into mine. "Stupid child! I haven't got anything for ten dollars."

"I'm sorry. I thought..."

"You thought, you thought!" He turned away and started counting the money from the cash register. I could see that he wanted to close the shop.

I felt my lips quivering. Nothing seemed to be working out the way I'd expected. The old man swept coins deftly into his hand, counting them as he went, then glanced up at me.

"Still here? All right. Give me what money you have." He took my crumpled ten dollars and put it in the cash box. "You'll have to pay the rest. One way or another. You understand that?"

"Yes! Thank you so much, Mr Owl. . . Mr Rowley!"

"No need to thank me. I said, you'll pay."

"Yes, of course I will!"

But how I was going to pay him I didn't know. I think I expected to do it by magic.

Mr Rowley unbolted the door and almost pushed me out. "Now go away!"

I couldn't wait to get home, but I forced myself to walk slowly – I was afraid of jolting things in the box. I couldn't afford anything to go wrong at this stage.

I wondered if the magic box had started working yet. Would there be a bag of money on my bed? Would Mum and Dad be there waiting for me?

But when I got home everything was exactly the same. Aunty Mona and Uncle Frank were in the living room playing one of their educational games, and a smell of boiling seaweed was coming from the kitchen.

Uncle Frank looked up as I came in. "What's that you've got, Cassidy?" he said.

I felt a bit shy about showing it to him, considering what I'd just been thinking. But I couldn't very well refuse, so I held the box up for him to see.

You would have thought I'd held up the Koh-i-noor diamond. Uncle Frank and Aunty

Mona both jumped to their feet and stood staring at the box in reverential wonder.

"Mona!" said Uncle Frank. "Look!"

"Yes, Frank. A Relative Enhancement Device!"

"A what?" I said.

"It's a kit," said Uncle Frank. "Your aunty and I put one together once, a long time ago."

A kit? It was supposed to be a magic box. Or at the very least, a video game. I put the box down on the coffee table. I had never been so disappointed in my life.

"I can't remember exactly what it did," said Aunty Mona. "But I do know that it was something interesting. Do you remember, Frank?"

Uncle Frank seemed uncomfortable, as if she had jogged a vague memory that wouldn't come into focus.

"Maybe," he said. "I remember an equalizing principle. That was very interesting – I wish I could remember why." He looked up and pulled out a chair.

"Anyway, Cassidy, are you ready?"

He opened his pocket-knife and cut off the wrapper. Then he carefully opened the lid.

It was definitely a kit. Set in little spaces in their styrofoam nest were glass tube-things, metal barrel-things, rolls of plastic-coated wire,

striped things of various colours, and a whole lot of other stuff that didn't look like anything at all. On the end of the box was a label that said "Batteries not included".

Uncle Frank and Aunty Mona exchanged glances again, and Aunty Mona gave him just the slightest nod. "These kits can be a bit tricky," said Uncle Frank, "if you don't know what you're doing. Your aunty and I have made one before. We'll give you a hand if you like."

"No, not me," said Aunty Mona "I know just how tricky those things can be." She seemed to be about to tell me something, but changed her mind and said, "Guess what, Cassidy? I know how much you like custard so I'm about to make some, out of soy milk and the air-bladder of a fish. Much healthier than the stuff you're used to!"

I wanted to say stop, please, I've given up dessert, but disappointment had filled my mouth with ashes. The magic video was just a kit! Worse than that – it was a kit so boring that my aunty and uncle had owned one.

"We'll check the parts list first," said Uncle Frank. While I stood numbly by, he found a list of parts and began checking ". . . Capacitors okay, plastic-coated wire okay, LEDs okay. . . Let's check this one: three double-looped

electron dividers, part numbers 186a, 186b, and 186c. Can you see them?"

I didn't know. Could I?

"There – next to the lepton mass simulator, number 23y."

Oh, good.

"And there's the left positronic field shunt, number 252x."

I'd never seen Uncle Frank like this before. He looked like Sam, his hair all ruffled, his face pink with excitement. Eagerly, he pointed things out and showed me how to put them together.

"Some parts you'll need to solder," he said. "I'll help you with that after dinner."

"Clear the table, you two!" called Aunty Mona from the kitchen. "Here comes dinner!"

"Yes, that's enough for now," said Uncle Frank. "Make sure you put it somewhere safe."

I carried the partly finished kit into my room and put it on my desk. As I set it down I had to dodge around Mephisto, who was sprawled across the desk, and the instruction book slipped off to one side. A piece of paper fluttered to the floor, but I didn't bother to pick it up. I am a naturally messy person.

But I did look at the instruction book. Up till now I hadn't been using it – Uncle Frank had been telling me what to do. But now, perhaps

to ease my disappointment, I felt like doing something for myself. I looked through the book until I found the part that we were up to.

The writing said: "Fit the flange of the lepton mass simulator (Tab F) into Slot G." So I did. Then I went to have dinner.

As I'd suspected, the boiled-seaweed smell turned out to be boiled seaweed. Aunty Mona ladled it onto our plates along with some half-cooked brown rice ("Rice should always be *al dente*," she said) and some fermented beans with sweet-and-sour sardines on top.

But it was the dessert I was dreading. Did the air-bladder of a fish mean we were having fish-flavoured custard?

I never got the chance to find out. We were just sitting down at the table again when there was a noise from my bedroom. It sounded like Mephisto jumping off my desk.

"Was that the cat?" asked Uncle Frank.

"Probably not," I said.

"It came from your bedroom, Cassidy," said Aunty Mona, standing up. "Is your cat in there? I'll be extremely disappointed if it is." And she marched down the hall and straight into my bedroom, ignoring all the signs on the door.

Mephisto shot out, hissing, and streaked into the kitchen, his fur standing out all over like a bunch of feather dusters.

"Cassidy," said Uncle Frank, "I thought we made it clear to you – you must keep your cat outside." And he followed Mephisto into the kitchen. And I followed Uncle Frank.

When I got to the kitchen I saw Mephisto under the table, growling and thrashing his tail. And Uncle Frank was staring, horrified, at something on the fridge.

"Mona?" he called. "Mona?" He turned to me. "Cassidy! The photonic energy tube! Cassidy! You didn't..."

"The what?"

"The photonic energy tube! Cassidy! Surely you didn't..." His voice trembled and faded away. And as I watched, the rest of him faded away too. One moment he was staring at the

fridge; the next, I could see through his shoes. One more moment, and he wasn't there at all.

"Aunty Mona!" I screeched. "Look at this!" What I expected her to look at I don't know; Uncle Frank hadn't left so much as a button. In fact, the whole house had become very quiet. I tiptoed into my bedroom, dreading what I might find.

Aunty Mona wasn't there. "Aunty Mona?" I called. No answer. I started searching the house, hunting through room after room, calling her name; and sometimes, for variety, I called Uncle Frank. But neither of them answered. They had definitely disappeared.

I didn't like the feeling. Annoying as my aunty and uncle were, they were better than no one at all. And tonight for a while they had seemed almost human. They must be in the house somewhere. I called them again. "Aunty Mona? Uncle Frank?" There was no sound.

Then I remembered – Uncle Frank had been looking at something on the fridge just before he disappeared. I went to the kitchen again; I wanted to see what it was that had upset him.

It upset me, too, when I found it. On the fridge was a familiar photo showing acres of shaved green lawn. That was all – just lawn. There was no one standing on it any more.

7

IMPORTANT WARNING

Losing the people who look after you is very unpleasant, even when you have been trying to lose them. It took me a long time to settle down and think what to do.

I decided I had better get in touch with an adult, someone who could look after me. My first thought was to call Vanessa's mother, because she always used to feed me so well. But then I remembered that I wasn't exactly on her good list; she probably wouldn't be very pleased to hear from me.

So I called Daniel's mother. She would know how to get in touch with our parents, and until they came home surely she would look after Mephisto and me.

"Mrs Fox," I said, trying to keep my voice from shaking, "it's Cassidy."

"Who?"

I thought she probably didn't recognize my voice. It sounded strange even to me.

"It's Cassidy. Sam's sister, " I said.

"Who's Sam?"

"My brother."

"Should I know him?"

"Are you Mrs. Fox?"

"Yes. Who are you?"

"Cassidy." This didn't seem to be working out. "I need to talk to Sam," I said, "or Daniel."

"You've got the wrong number. There's no Sam or Daniel here."

"Are you sure?"

I suppose she must have been, because she hung up.

Losing an aunty and uncle was one thing. Losing Sam was another. I'd been feeling quite kindly toward Sam lately, and I certainly didn't want to lose him altogether. I went into my bedroom, my feet feeling strangely heavy.

I called Mephisto, but he wouldn't come. So I crawled into bed alone, and it was then that I saw the slip of paper. It read:

IMPORTANT WARNING! In models IIIE and IVE, soon after the flange of the lepton mass simulator (Tab F) is fitted into Slot G, the photonic energy tube will activate and Goldberg's Equalizing Principle will come into operation. To avoid unintended effects, once this stage of assembly is

reached, the Relative Enhancement Device should be kept in a safe place.

For once in my life, I really wished I'd been a tidy person.

I looked at the assembly. If fitting two pieces together had caused all this, would undoing them make things go back to normal again? The answer was no.

The bits that had slipped together so easily were clearly not meant to come apart. They were seamlessly bonded.

I looked at the instruction book. If I could finish assembling whatever it was, perhaps I could reverse the effects? But I had no hope of finishing it – the instructions were full of strange symbols and diagrams that made no sense at all to me.

I needed to find an adult. Perhaps I could call Vanessa's parents and try to explain things. They might think differently if they heard my side of the story.

But when I spoke to Vanessa's mother, I got the same response I'd had from Mrs Fox. She'd never heard of anyone named Vanessa. Worse still, she had never heard of anyone named Cassidy.

I got into my parents' bed and sat with the phone on my lap. But I couldn't think who else to call. Except for the police. Didn't people call the police when someone was lost? But what would the police do? Would they take me away and put me in a home? And what would happen to Mephisto?

That reminded me, it was time to feed him, but for the first time since Mephisto came to us, I wasn't looking forward to it. I just wanted to curl up and sleep. But Mephisto needed me to look after him, so I forced myself to get up and go to the kitchen. I even got some comfort out of opening a can of sardines for him. At least Mephisto was going to be all right; there were enough sardines to last the rest of his life.

At the sound of the can being opened Mephisto should have come running. But he didn't.

Filled with a dreadful foreboding, I walked through the house calling him. There was no answering meow, and finally I had to believe it: Mephisto had disappeared, too!

I wondered where Mum and Dad were, and what they would think when they found out what I'd done. If they ever did find out, that is. They had to come home first.

The postcard! I could steam the stamps off and see what was written underneath. It might give me some clue to where they were. Maybe I could find out where to call them. I wasn't at all looking forward to telling them that I'd dematerialised their only son, and Dad's only brother, not to mention the family's only pet. But it was better than being all alone. I put the kettle on and got the postcard out of my bag.

But when I went to steam the stamps off, I saw there was no point: the stamps weren't covering the writing any more. There was no writing. Except for the picture and the stamps, the postcard was completely blank. So Mum and Dad were gone, too. I was uncleless, auntyless, brotherless, friendless, catless, and an orphan.

At that moment I would have given anything to have even my boring, stuffy uncle back. I wished I'd listened to his lectures on money. I would still have borrowed, of course, but maybe I'd feel better about it. His favourite saying slipped into my mind: "Take what you want, and pay for it." I supposed that's what I was doing now.

Of course! That's what the old man in the shop had said: one way or another I would pay for the thing I'd bought. That was Goldberg's Equalizing Principle! *One way or another* I would pay, either with money or – family.

To get my family back, maybe all I had to do was pay the old man what I owed him. Frantically I searched the house. But every sign of my aunty and uncle had vanished – including Aunty Mona's purse. That seemed unfair to me. It might have been her purse, but it had my pocket money in it.

I went on looking. All I needed was twenty dollars. Then I'd go to the shop and make Mr Rowley give my family back. If he wouldn't, I'd make him look after me.

I searched the house until late into the night, but I didn't find a single coin. I fell asleep on the couch, with the television hissing and all the lights turned on for company.

8

PAYBACK

I woke up much earlier than I usually do, and for an instant I thought I was in my own bed, with Mephisto in the bend of my knees, and everything as it ought to be.

But then I remembered what had happened, and how I was a victim of a photonic energy tube, Goldberg's Equalizing Principle, and my own messy habits.

I started to put some sardines in Mephisto's dish, but then I remembered that he had disappeared, too. I put his dish in a cupboard where I wouldn't have to look at it.

I started my fruitless search for money again, because I couldn't think of anything else to do. But as I was rummaging through the drawers and cupboards, another idea occurred to me.

I could take the kit back. I couldn't dismantle it, of course. But I could take the whole thing to the shop. I could point out that it was faulty, and that I should have a refund. Then it would be *me* owed something: my family, and with a bit of luck my ten dollars, too, but I wouldn't quibble over that.

I found a plastic bag in the kitchen drawer. It was brilliant pink, with "Linda's Hair and Nails" printed on it in big curly letters. To make the kit safer to carry – I didn't want any more unintended effects – I put the bag in a carton that had once held 144 cans of sardines. And just before nine, I set off for the Magic Shop.

But when I got to Hale Street, I found something else unexpected. Or rather, I *didn't* find it! The Magic Shop had disappeared, too. It had turned into something else. Overnight, the building had become bright pink, and now a pink and white sign announced "Linda's Hair and Nails" in gigantic curly letters.

The only person inside was a woman with plum-coloured hair. She was sitting at a bright pink counter, painting her nails bright pink to match. There was no sign of the old man.

I marched into the shop and put my box down on the counter. "This belongs to you."

"No it doesn't." The woman didn't even look up, and went on putting on her nail polish. She did it very elegantly, with long, sweeping strokes. "We didn't order anything."

"Have it anyway."

"We don't want it."

A lady with shoulder-length brown hair came in for a haircut. She wanted it very short. The plum-coloured hairdresser clipped away for a while, and the woman kept saying, "Take a bit more off" until in the end the floor was scattered with hair snippings, and the woman looked like a monkey.

But at last I knew what to do. I grabbed a broom and started sweeping up the hair clippings. While I was still doing that another woman came in for a haircut, and I swept up her hair, too.

At last the hairdresser looked at me. "You can make me a cup of coffee, then straighten up the boxes in the back room."

Another hairdresser, a pink-haired one this time, turned up for work. Apparently the salon was very busy this morning. I swept, fetched and carried, and made endless cups of coffee.

Just before lunch-time, the plum-coloured hairdresser said, "You can finish up now."

I wasn't sure if I'd done enough. There'd been no sign that anything was changing. "Are you sure?" I said. "I'll clean the windows if you like." The hairdresser shrugged and handed me a bucket and cloth.

I had cleaned about a quarter of one window when a short girl with stringy hair and pink and white tennis shoes walked in.

"Vanessa!" I yelled. "What are you doing here?" And I punched her to show how pleased I was.

Vanessa seemed puzzled. "Getting my hair done for the wedding. I'm having all these curls down the sides, and little pink roses..."

I ran all the way home. I still didn't know if my idea had worked completely – maybe I'd only paid for Vanessa. But I had to see.

When I got home Mephisto came running to meet me, twining himself around my legs, meowing to be fed. I wanted to give him the sardines from the morning, but I couldn't find them. So I gave him a piece of roast chicken from the fridge.

There was still no sign of Aunty Mona or Uncle Frank. But then I heard laughter.

"Well, Cassidy," said Uncle Frank as he walked in, "let's get rid of this heavy stuff in my pocket." He gave me a handful of coins.

Behind him fluttered Aunty Mona in a coffee-coloured polyester dress. "Cassidy, darling," she said, "you'd better have this. It's only glass, but it'll look better on you." And she handed me a glittering green brooch.

Mum and Dad came home two days later. They had decided to come back early because of unexpected heavy snowfalls in Vienna.

"So how did you get along, Chicken Casserole?" asked Mum. "You must have had a good time – you didn't call us once."

Aunty Mona and Uncle Frank stayed on a few more days. We had a lot of fun together, and when it was time for them to leave I helped them to pack up.

But when I went to pack the thermos flask Aunty Mona stopped me.

"Don't bother," she said. "You keep it for picnics. Frank and I'll have something on the plane."

I knew then how much they'd changed. The couple whose cases I helped carry out to Dad's car were not the same people as the couple who'd come to visit.

I mentioned it to Mum as we went out to the car. "You noticed, didn't you? The night they turned up you said how different they were."

"A few years ago," Mum said, "your aunty and uncle suddenly got rich. No one knew exactly how – we thought it must have been a lottery or something. But we did hear afterwards that having money had changed them, and when they turned up here we knew it must be true. They just weren't themselves any more."

"But," Dad added cheerfully, "the holiday with you seems to have worked like magic. They're quite the old Frank and Mona again, aren't they? And of course the story about the lottery was all rubbish. They're not rich at all."

"Don't they have a huge garden with rolling green lawns?"

"They work at a country club," said Mum. "Uncle Frank is the gardener and Aunty Mona is the cook."

So that was what the Relative Enhancement Device did: it enhanced relatives! And the Equalizing Principle made sure they paid for it.

What a lucky escape I'd had! I hadn't changed at all. I was sure.

I still thought all that magic stuff was babyish. And I still liked cabbage and sardine stew better than a hamburger any day.

TITLES IN THE SERIES

SET 9A

Television Drama
Time for Sale
The Shady Deal
The Loch Ness Monster Mystery
Secrets of the Desert

SET 9B

To JJ From CC
Pandora's Box
The Birthday Disaster
The Song of the Mantis
Helping the Hoiho

SET 9C

Glumly
Rupert and the Griffin
The Tree, the Trunk, and the Tuba
Errol the Peril
Cassidy's Magic

SET 9D

Barney
Get a Grip, Pip!
Casey's Case
Dear Future
Strange Meetings

SET 10A

A Battle of Words
The Rainbow Solution
Fortune's Friend
Eureka
It's a Frog's Life

SET 10B

The Cat Burglar of Pethaven Drive
The Matchbox
In Search of the Great Bears
Many Happy Returns
Spider Relatives

SET 10C

Horrible Hank
Brian's Brilliant Career
Fernitickles
It's All in Your Mind, James Robert
Wing High, Gooftah

SET 10D

The Week of the Jellyhoppers
Timothy Whuffenpuffen-Whippersnapper
Timedetectors
Ryan's Dog Ringo
The Secret of Kiribu Tapu Lagoon